50 Delicious Winter Comfort Foods Recipes

By: Kelly Johnson

Table of Contents

- Classic Beef Stew
- Chicken Pot Pie
- Creamy Macaroni and Cheese
- Baked Ziti with Meatballs
- Shepherd's Pie
- Chicken and Dumplings
- Beef Stroganoff
- Roasted Root Vegetables
- Lasagna with Garlic Bread
- Slow Cooker Chili
- Creamy Tomato Soup with Grilled Cheese
- Baked Potato Soup
- Sausage and Potato Casserole
- Meatloaf with Mashed Potatoes
- Homemade Chicken Noodle Soup
- Chicken Alfredo Bake
- Beef and Ale Pie
- Cheesy Scalloped Potatoes
- Sweet Potato Casserole
- Slow-Cooked Ribs
- Pumpkin Risotto
- Stuffed Bell Peppers
- Braised Short Ribs with Mashed Potatoes
- Goulash
- Swedish Meatballs with Gravy
- Beef Wellington
- Fried Chicken with Gravy
- Chicken Parmesan
- Eggplant Parmesan
- Beef and Bean Burritos
- Grilled Cheese and Tomato Soup
- Clam Chowder
- Pork Schnitzel with Cabbage
- Baked French Onion Soup
- Roasted Chicken with Root Vegetables

- Sweet and Sour Meatballs
- Baked Mac and Cheese with Bacon
- Cozy Risotto with Mushrooms
- Braised Lamb Shanks
- Sloppy Joes
- Cornbread with Chili
- Baked Chicken Thighs with Garlic Butter
- Stuffed Mushrooms with Cream Cheese
- Cabbage Rolls
- Baked Salmon with Lemon Dill Sauce
- Chicken Enchiladas with Sour Cream
- Creamed Spinach
- Poutine
- Slow-Cooked Pork Carnitas
- Homemade Biscuits with Gravy

Classic Beef Stew

Ingredients:

- 2 tablespoons olive oil
- 2 pounds beef stew meat, cut into cubes
- Salt and pepper to taste
- 1 onion, chopped
- 3 garlic cloves, minced
- 3 carrots, peeled and sliced
- 2 potatoes, peeled and cubed
- 3 cups beef broth
- 1 cup red wine
- 2 tablespoons tomato paste
- 2 teaspoons dried thyme
- 1 teaspoon dried rosemary
- 1 bay leaf
- 1 cup frozen peas

Instructions:

1. Heat olive oil in a large pot over medium-high heat. Season the beef with salt and pepper, and brown in batches, about 5 minutes per batch. Remove the beef and set it aside.
2. Add the onion and garlic to the pot and sauté for 3 minutes until softened.
3. Add the tomato paste, carrots, potatoes, beef broth, red wine, thyme, rosemary, and bay leaf. Stir to combine.
4. Bring to a boil, then reduce heat to low. Cover and simmer for 1.5 to 2 hours, or until the beef is tender.
5. Stir in the peas and cook for an additional 5 minutes. Adjust seasoning with salt and pepper before serving.

Chicken Pot Pie

Ingredients:

- 2 tablespoons butter
- 1 onion, chopped
- 2 carrots, diced
- 2 celery stalks, chopped
- 2 garlic cloves, minced
- 1/3 cup all-purpose flour
- 2 1/2 cups chicken broth
- 1 cup milk
- 3 cups cooked chicken, shredded
- 1 cup frozen peas
- Salt and pepper to taste
- 2 sheets puff pastry or pie dough

Instructions:

1. Preheat the oven to 400°F (200°C).
2. In a large skillet, melt butter over medium heat. Add the onion, carrots, celery, and garlic, and cook for 5 minutes until softened.
3. Stir in the flour and cook for 1 minute. Gradually add the chicken broth and milk, stirring constantly until thickened.
4. Add the shredded chicken, peas, salt, and pepper. Stir to combine.
5. Roll out the puff pastry or pie dough and line a 9-inch pie dish. Pour the chicken mixture into the dish and top with another sheet of dough. Trim any excess dough and crimp the edges to seal.
6. Cut a few slits in the top of the pie to allow steam to escape.
7. Bake for 30-35 minutes, or until the crust is golden brown. Let it cool for 5 minutes before serving.

Creamy Macaroni and Cheese

Ingredients:

- 8 ounces elbow macaroni
- 2 tablespoons butter
- 2 tablespoons all-purpose flour
- 2 cups milk
- 2 cups shredded sharp cheddar cheese
- 1/2 cup grated Parmesan cheese
- Salt and pepper to taste
- 1/4 teaspoon paprika (optional)

Instructions:

1. Cook the macaroni according to package instructions, drain, and set aside.
2. In a large saucepan, melt butter over medium heat. Whisk in the flour and cook for 1 minute until lightly golden.
3. Gradually add the milk, whisking constantly to avoid lumps. Cook for 5-7 minutes until the sauce thickens.
4. Stir in the cheddar cheese, Parmesan, salt, pepper, and paprika (if using). Cook until the cheese melts and the sauce is smooth.
5. Add the cooked macaroni to the sauce and stir to coat. Serve warm.

Baked Ziti with Meatballs

Ingredients:

- 1 pound ziti pasta
- 2 tablespoons olive oil
- 1 onion, chopped
- 2 garlic cloves, minced
- 1 jar marinara sauce (24 ounces)
- 1/2 cup ricotta cheese
- 2 cups shredded mozzarella cheese
- 1/4 cup grated Parmesan cheese
- 1/4 teaspoon dried oregano
- 1/4 teaspoon dried basil
- 12-15 meatballs (store-bought or homemade)

Instructions:

1. Preheat the oven to 375°F (190°C).
2. Cook the ziti according to package instructions. Drain and set aside.
3. In a large skillet, heat olive oil over medium heat. Add the onion and garlic and sauté for 5 minutes until softened.
4. Stir in the marinara sauce, ricotta cheese, mozzarella, Parmesan, oregano, and basil. Add the cooked ziti and meatballs, and stir to combine.
5. Pour the mixture into a baking dish and sprinkle with additional mozzarella and Parmesan cheese.
6. Bake for 20-25 minutes, until the cheese is melted and bubbly. Serve hot.

Shepherd's Pie

Ingredients:

- 2 tablespoons olive oil
- 1 onion, chopped
- 2 garlic cloves, minced
- 1 pound ground beef or lamb
- 2 carrots, diced
- 1 cup frozen peas
- 1/4 cup tomato paste
- 1 cup beef broth
- 2 tablespoons Worcestershire sauce
- 4 cups mashed potatoes (prepared)
- Salt and pepper to taste

Instructions:

1. Preheat the oven to 400°F (200°C).
2. In a large skillet, heat olive oil over medium heat. Add the onion and garlic, and cook for 3 minutes.
3. Add the ground beef or lamb and cook until browned. Drain any excess fat.
4. Stir in the carrots, peas, tomato paste, beef broth, Worcestershire sauce, salt, and pepper. Simmer for 10 minutes until the mixture thickens.
5. Transfer the meat mixture to a baking dish and top with mashed potatoes. Spread the potatoes evenly over the top.
6. Bake for 20 minutes, or until the top is golden and crispy. Serve hot.

Chicken and Dumplings

Ingredients:

- 1 tablespoon olive oil
- 1 onion, chopped
- 2 carrots, diced
- 2 celery stalks, chopped
- 3 garlic cloves, minced
- 4 cups chicken broth
- 1/2 cup heavy cream
- 3 cups cooked chicken, shredded
- Salt and pepper to taste

For the Dumplings:

- 1 cup all-purpose flour
- 1 teaspoon baking powder
- 1/4 teaspoon salt
- 1/2 cup milk
- 1 tablespoon butter, melted
- 1 teaspoon dried thyme

Instructions:

1. In a large pot, heat olive oil over medium heat. Add the onion, carrots, celery, and garlic, and cook for 5 minutes until softened.
2. Add the chicken broth and heavy cream, and bring to a simmer.
3. Stir in the cooked chicken and season with salt and pepper. Keep warm.
4. For the dumplings, mix the flour, baking powder, salt, milk, butter, and thyme in a bowl until just combined.
5. Drop spoonfuls of the dumpling batter into the simmering soup. Cover and cook for 15 minutes, until the dumplings are cooked through.
6. Serve hot.

Beef Stroganoff

Ingredients:

- 1 tablespoon olive oil
- 1 pound beef sirloin, sliced thinly
- Salt and pepper to taste
- 1 onion, chopped
- 2 garlic cloves, minced
- 1 cup beef broth
- 1 tablespoon Dijon mustard
- 1/2 cup sour cream
- 1 tablespoon flour
- 1/4 cup fresh parsley, chopped

Instructions:

1. Heat olive oil in a large skillet over medium heat. Season the beef with salt and pepper and cook in batches until browned. Remove the beef and set aside.
2. In the same skillet, add the onion and garlic, and sauté for 3 minutes until softened.
3. Add the beef broth and Dijon mustard, stirring to combine. Simmer for 5 minutes.
4. Stir in the sour cream and flour, cooking until thickened, about 2-3 minutes.
5. Return the beef to the skillet and cook for another 2-3 minutes. Garnish with parsley before serving.

Roasted Root Vegetables

Ingredients:

- 2 carrots, peeled and sliced
- 2 parsnips, peeled and sliced
- 1 sweet potato, peeled and cubed
- 1 rutabaga, peeled and cubed
- 2 tablespoons olive oil
- Salt and pepper to taste
- 1 teaspoon dried thyme
- 1 teaspoon dried rosemary

Instructions:

1. Preheat the oven to 400°F (200°C).
2. Toss the carrots, parsnips, sweet potato, and rutabaga with olive oil, salt, pepper, thyme, and rosemary.
3. Spread the vegetables evenly on a baking sheet and roast for 25-30 minutes, or until tender and golden.
4. Serve warm as a side dish.

Lasagna with Garlic Bread

Ingredients:

For the Lasagna:

- 12 lasagna noodles
- 2 tablespoons olive oil
- 1 pound ground beef
- 1 onion, chopped
- 2 garlic cloves, minced
- 2 cups ricotta cheese
- 1 egg
- 4 cups shredded mozzarella cheese
- 1 cup grated Parmesan cheese
- 3 cups marinara sauce
- Salt and pepper to taste
- 1 teaspoon dried oregano
- 1 teaspoon dried basil

For the Garlic Bread:

- 1 loaf French bread
- 1/2 cup butter, softened
- 3 garlic cloves, minced
- 1 tablespoon chopped fresh parsley
- 1/4 teaspoon salt

Instructions:

1. Preheat the oven to 375°F (190°C).
2. Cook the lasagna noodles according to package instructions. Drain and set aside.
3. Heat olive oil in a large skillet over medium heat. Add the ground beef, onion, and garlic, and cook until the beef is browned. Drain excess fat and stir in marinara sauce, oregano, and basil. Simmer for 10 minutes.
4. In a bowl, combine ricotta cheese, egg, 1 cup of mozzarella, and Parmesan cheese. Season with salt and pepper.
5. In a baking dish, spread a thin layer of sauce, followed by a layer of noodles, ricotta mixture, and mozzarella. Repeat the layers, finishing with mozzarella on top.

6. Cover with foil and bake for 30 minutes. Remove the foil and bake for another 10 minutes, until the cheese is bubbly and golden.
7. For the garlic bread, slice the French bread in half lengthwise. Mix the softened butter, garlic, parsley, and salt. Spread evenly on the bread halves and bake for 10-12 minutes, until golden brown.
8. Serve the lasagna with the garlic bread.

Slow Cooker Chili

Ingredients:

- 1 pound ground beef
- 1 onion, chopped
- 1 bell pepper, chopped
- 2 garlic cloves, minced
- 1 can (15 ounces) kidney beans, drained and rinsed
- 1 can (15 ounces) black beans, drained and rinsed
- 1 can (15 ounces) diced tomatoes
- 1 can (6 ounces) tomato paste
- 1 can (4 ounces) green chilies, diced
- 2 tablespoons chili powder
- 1 teaspoon cumin
- 1 teaspoon paprika
- Salt and pepper to taste

Instructions:

1. In a skillet, brown the ground beef over medium heat. Drain the fat and transfer the beef to a slow cooker.
2. Add the onion, bell pepper, garlic, beans, diced tomatoes, tomato paste, green chilies, chili powder, cumin, paprika, salt, and pepper to the slow cooker. Stir to combine.
3. Cover and cook on low for 6-8 hours or on high for 3-4 hours.
4. Serve hot, with optional toppings like sour cream, shredded cheese, or chopped green onions.

Creamy Tomato Soup with Grilled Cheese

Ingredients:

For the Tomato Soup:

- 2 tablespoons olive oil
- 1 onion, chopped
- 3 garlic cloves, minced
- 1 can (28 ounces) crushed tomatoes
- 2 cups chicken broth
- 1 cup heavy cream
- Salt and pepper to taste
- 1/2 teaspoon dried basil

For the Grilled Cheese:

- 8 slices bread
- 4 tablespoons butter, softened
- 8 slices cheddar cheese

Instructions:

1. For the soup, heat olive oil in a pot over medium heat. Add the onion and garlic, cooking for 5 minutes until softened.
2. Stir in the crushed tomatoes, chicken broth, salt, pepper, and basil. Bring to a simmer and cook for 15 minutes.
3. Stir in the heavy cream and cook for another 5 minutes. Use an immersion blender to blend until smooth (optional).
4. For the grilled cheese, butter one side of each slice of bread. Place cheese between two slices and grill in a skillet over medium heat until golden and cheese is melted, about 3-4 minutes per side.
5. Serve the soup hot with grilled cheese sandwiches on the side.

Baked Potato Soup

Ingredients:

- 4 large russet potatoes, peeled and cubed
- 4 cups chicken broth
- 1 onion, chopped
- 3 garlic cloves, minced
- 1/2 cup heavy cream
- 1 cup shredded cheddar cheese
- 1/4 cup sour cream
- Salt and pepper to taste
- Green onions and bacon bits for topping

Instructions:

1. In a large pot, add the cubed potatoes and chicken broth. Bring to a boil, then reduce heat and simmer for 15 minutes, until the potatoes are tender.
2. In a separate pan, sauté the onion and garlic in a bit of olive oil for 5 minutes until softened.
3. Add the sautéed onion and garlic to the pot with the potatoes. Stir in the heavy cream, cheddar cheese, sour cream, salt, and pepper.
4. Use a potato masher or immersion blender to mash the potatoes to your desired consistency.
5. Serve hot, topped with green onions and bacon bits.

Sausage and Potato Casserole

Ingredients:

- 1 pound sausage, crumbled
- 4 large potatoes, peeled and sliced
- 1 onion, chopped
- 2 cups shredded cheese (cheddar or mozzarella)
- 1/2 cup heavy cream
- Salt and pepper to taste

Instructions:

1. Preheat the oven to 375°F (190°C).
2. In a skillet, cook the sausage over medium heat until browned. Remove excess fat.
3. In a greased baking dish, layer the sliced potatoes, sausage, onion, and cheese. Season with salt and pepper.
4. Pour the heavy cream over the casserole and cover with foil.
5. Bake for 45 minutes, then uncover and bake for another 15 minutes, until the potatoes are tender and the top is golden.

Meatloaf with Mashed Potatoes

Ingredients:

For the Meatloaf:

- 1 1/2 pounds ground beef
- 1/2 cup breadcrumbs
- 1/4 cup milk
- 1 egg
- 1 onion, chopped
- 1/4 cup ketchup
- 2 tablespoons Worcestershire sauce
- 1 teaspoon dried oregano
- Salt and pepper to taste

For the Mashed Potatoes:

- 4 large potatoes, peeled and cubed
- 1/2 cup butter
- 1/2 cup milk
- Salt and pepper to taste

Instructions:

1. Preheat the oven to 375°F (190°C).
2. For the meatloaf, mix the ground beef, breadcrumbs, milk, egg, onion, ketchup, Worcestershire sauce, oregano, salt, and pepper in a large bowl. Form into a loaf shape and place in a baking dish.
3. Bake for 45-50 minutes, or until the meatloaf is cooked through.
4. For the mashed potatoes, boil the potatoes in salted water for 15-20 minutes, until tender. Drain and mash with butter, milk, salt, and pepper.
5. Serve the meatloaf with mashed potatoes on the side.

Homemade Chicken Noodle Soup

Ingredients:

- 1 tablespoon olive oil
- 1 onion, chopped
- 2 carrots, diced
- 2 celery stalks, chopped
- 3 garlic cloves, minced
- 6 cups chicken broth
- 2 cups cooked chicken, shredded
- 2 cups egg noodles
- Salt and pepper to taste
- Fresh parsley for garnish

Instructions:

1. In a large pot, heat olive oil over medium heat. Add the onion, carrots, celery, and garlic, and sauté for 5 minutes.
2. Add the chicken broth and bring to a boil. Reduce heat and simmer for 10 minutes.
3. Stir in the shredded chicken, egg noodles, salt, and pepper. Cook for 8-10 minutes until the noodles are tender.
4. Serve hot, garnished with fresh parsley.

Chicken Alfredo Bake

Ingredients:

- 2 cups cooked chicken, shredded
- 12 oz penne pasta
- 2 cups Alfredo sauce
- 1 cup shredded mozzarella cheese
- 1/2 cup grated Parmesan cheese
- Salt and pepper to taste

Instructions:

1. Preheat the oven to 375°F (190°C).
2. Cook the penne pasta according to package instructions. Drain and set aside.
3. In a large mixing bowl, combine the cooked chicken, pasta, Alfredo sauce, mozzarella, Parmesan, salt, and pepper. Stir to combine.
4. Transfer the mixture to a greased baking dish and top with extra mozzarella.
5. Bake for 20-25 minutes, until the cheese is melted and bubbly.

Beef and Ale Pie

Ingredients:

- 1 pound beef stew meat, cut into cubes
- 2 tablespoons olive oil
- 1 onion, chopped
- 2 carrots, diced
- 2 garlic cloves, minced
- 1 cup ale
- 1 cup beef broth
- 1 tablespoon tomato paste
- 1 teaspoon dried thyme
- Salt and pepper to taste
- 1 package puff pastry
- 1 egg (for egg wash)

Instructions:

1. Preheat the oven to 400°F (200°C).
2. Heat olive oil in a large pot over medium heat. Brown the beef in batches, then remove and set aside.
3. Add the onion, carrots, and garlic to the pot and sauté for 5 minutes. Stir in the tomato paste and cook for 1 minute.
4. Add the ale, beef broth, thyme, salt, and pepper. Return the beef to the pot and simmer for 1 hour, until the beef is tender.
5. Roll out the puff pastry and cut to fit your pie dish. Place the mixture in the dish and cover with pastry.
6. Brush with an egg wash and bake for 20-25 minutes, until the pastry is golden brown.

Cheesy Scalloped Potatoes

Ingredients:

- 6 large russet potatoes, peeled and thinly sliced
- 2 cups shredded cheddar cheese
- 1 cup heavy cream
- 1 cup milk
- 2 tablespoons butter
- 2 garlic cloves, minced
- 1/2 teaspoon salt
- 1/4 teaspoon pepper
- 1/2 teaspoon dried thyme
- 1/4 cup grated Parmesan cheese

Instructions:

1. Preheat the oven to 375°F (190°C). Grease a 9x13-inch baking dish with butter or cooking spray.
2. In a saucepan, melt the butter over medium heat. Add the minced garlic and cook for 1 minute until fragrant.
3. Add the heavy cream, milk, salt, pepper, and thyme. Stir and cook until heated through.
4. Layer half of the sliced potatoes in the prepared baking dish. Pour half of the cream mixture over the potatoes and sprinkle with half of the cheddar cheese. Repeat with another layer of potatoes, cream mixture, and cheese.
5. Top with Parmesan cheese.
6. Cover with foil and bake for 45 minutes. Remove the foil and bake for an additional 20 minutes, or until the potatoes are tender and the cheese is bubbly and golden.
7. Let it rest for a few minutes before serving.

Sweet Potato Casserole

Ingredients:

- 4 large sweet potatoes, peeled and cubed
- 1/2 cup brown sugar
- 1/2 cup butter, softened
- 1 teaspoon vanilla extract
- 1/2 cup milk
- 2 eggs
- 1/2 teaspoon cinnamon
- 1/4 teaspoon nutmeg
- 1 cup mini marshmallows (optional)

Instructions:

1. Preheat the oven to 350°F (175°C). Grease a 9x13-inch baking dish.
2. Boil the sweet potatoes in salted water until tender, about 15 minutes. Drain and mash.
3. In a large mixing bowl, combine the mashed sweet potatoes, brown sugar, butter, vanilla, milk, eggs, cinnamon, and nutmeg. Mix well until smooth.
4. Transfer the mixture to the prepared baking dish and smooth out the top.
5. (Optional) Top with mini marshmallows and bake for 25-30 minutes, or until golden and bubbling.
6. Serve warm as a side dish.

Slow-Cooked Ribs

Ingredients:

- 2 racks baby back ribs
- 1/2 cup BBQ sauce
- 2 tablespoons brown sugar
- 1 tablespoon paprika
- 1 tablespoon garlic powder
- 1 teaspoon onion powder
- 1 teaspoon salt
- 1/2 teaspoon black pepper
- 1/2 teaspoon cayenne pepper (optional)

Instructions:

1. Preheat the slow cooker on low.
2. Mix the brown sugar, paprika, garlic powder, onion powder, salt, black pepper, and cayenne pepper (if using) in a small bowl.
3. Rub the spice mixture generously over both sides of the ribs.
4. Place the ribs in the slow cooker, meat side up, and cover with the lid.
5. Cook for 6-8 hours, until the ribs are tender and falling off the bone.
6. Preheat your grill or broiler.
7. Remove the ribs from the slow cooker and brush with BBQ sauce.
8. Grill or broil the ribs for 3-5 minutes on each side to caramelize the sauce. Serve hot.

Pumpkin Risotto

Ingredients:

- 1 cup Arborio rice
- 1 can (15 ounces) pure pumpkin puree
- 4 cups chicken or vegetable broth, warm
- 1/2 cup dry white wine
- 1/2 onion, chopped
- 2 tablespoons butter
- 1/2 cup Parmesan cheese
- 1/2 teaspoon ground cinnamon
- Salt and pepper to taste

Instructions:

1. In a large skillet, melt the butter over medium heat. Add the chopped onion and cook until softened, about 5 minutes.
2. Stir in the Arborio rice and cook for 2 minutes until the rice is lightly toasted.
3. Add the white wine and cook, stirring constantly, until the wine is mostly absorbed.
4. Gradually add the warm broth, one ladle at a time, stirring constantly. Wait until the liquid is absorbed before adding more broth.
5. After about 15 minutes, add the pumpkin puree and cinnamon. Continue to cook and add broth until the rice is tender and creamy, about 20-25 minutes.
6. Stir in Parmesan cheese, salt, and pepper.
7. Serve hot, garnished with additional Parmesan if desired.

Stuffed Bell Peppers

Ingredients:

- 4 large bell peppers, tops cut off and seeds removed
- 1 pound ground beef or turkey
- 1 cup cooked rice
- 1 can (15 ounces) tomato sauce
- 1 small onion, chopped
- 1 cup shredded cheese (cheddar, mozzarella, or a blend)
- 1 teaspoon garlic powder
- 1 teaspoon dried oregano
- Salt and pepper to taste

Instructions:

1. Preheat the oven to 375°F (190°C).
2. In a large skillet, cook the ground meat over medium heat until browned. Add the chopped onion and cook until softened.
3. Stir in the cooked rice, tomato sauce, garlic powder, oregano, salt, and pepper. Mix well and cook for 5-7 minutes until heated through.
4. Stuff the bell peppers with the mixture and place them in a baking dish.
5. Top with shredded cheese and cover the dish with foil.
6. Bake for 30 minutes. Remove the foil and bake for an additional 10 minutes to melt the cheese and finish cooking.
7. Serve hot.

Braised Short Ribs with Mashed Potatoes

Ingredients:

For the Short Ribs:

- 4 bone-in beef short ribs
- 2 tablespoons olive oil
- 1 onion, chopped
- 2 carrots, peeled and chopped
- 2 celery stalks, chopped
- 4 garlic cloves, minced
- 1 cup red wine
- 2 cups beef broth
- 2 sprigs fresh thyme
- 1 bay leaf
- Salt and pepper to taste

For the Mashed Potatoes:

- 6 large potatoes, peeled and cubed
- 1/2 cup butter
- 1/2 cup milk
- Salt and pepper to taste

Instructions:

1. Preheat the oven to 350°F (175°C).
2. In a large oven-safe pot, heat olive oil over medium-high heat. Season the short ribs with salt and pepper and sear on all sides until browned, about 10 minutes. Remove and set aside.
3. Add the chopped onion, carrots, celery, and garlic to the pot. Cook for 5-7 minutes, until softened.
4. Pour in the red wine and scrape up any browned bits from the bottom of the pot. Add the beef broth, thyme, and bay leaf. Return the short ribs to the pot.
5. Cover and braise in the oven for 2.5-3 hours, until the meat is tender and falling off the bone.
6. For the mashed potatoes, boil the potatoes in salted water for 15 minutes, until tender. Drain and mash with butter, milk, salt, and pepper.
7. Serve the short ribs on top of mashed potatoes.

Goulash

Ingredients:

- 1 pound beef stew meat
- 1 onion, chopped
- 2 garlic cloves, minced
- 1 can (14 ounces) diced tomatoes
- 1 cup beef broth
- 2 teaspoons paprika
- 1 teaspoon dried oregano
- 1 cup elbow macaroni
- Salt and pepper to taste

Instructions:

1. In a large pot, brown the beef stew meat over medium heat. Add the onion and garlic, cooking until softened.
2. Stir in the diced tomatoes, beef broth, paprika, oregano, salt, and pepper. Bring to a simmer.
3. Add the elbow macaroni and cook for 10-12 minutes, until the pasta is tender and the flavors have melded together.
4. Serve hot.

Swedish Meatballs with Gravy

Ingredients:

For the Meatballs:

- 1 pound ground beef
- 1/2 pound ground pork
- 1/4 cup breadcrumbs
- 1/4 cup milk
- 1 egg
- 1/2 onion, finely chopped
- Salt and pepper to taste

For the Gravy:

- 2 tablespoons butter
- 2 tablespoons flour
- 2 cups beef broth
- 1/2 cup heavy cream
- Salt and pepper to taste

Instructions:

1. Preheat the oven to 375°F (190°C).
2. In a mixing bowl, combine the beef, pork, breadcrumbs, milk, egg, onion, salt, and pepper. Form into small meatballs and place them on a baking sheet.
3. Bake the meatballs for 20-25 minutes, or until fully cooked.
4. For the gravy, melt butter in a pan over medium heat. Stir in the flour and cook for 1-2 minutes.
5. Gradually whisk in the beef broth and bring to a simmer. Stir in the heavy cream and cook until thickened.
6. Season the gravy with salt and pepper.
7. Serve the meatballs with the gravy.

Beef Wellington

Ingredients:

- 2 pounds beef tenderloin
- 2 tablespoons olive oil
- Salt and pepper to taste
- 8 ounces mushrooms, chopped
- 1 tablespoon butter
- 1/4 cup Dijon mustard
- 1 sheet puff pastry
- 1 egg, beaten

Instructions:

1. Preheat the oven to 400°F (200°C).
2. Season the beef tenderloin with salt and pepper. Heat olive oil in a skillet over high heat. Sear the beef on all sides until browned.
3. Brush the beef with Dijon mustard and set aside.
4. In the same skillet, sauté the mushrooms in butter until soft, about 5-7 minutes. Allow to cool.
5. Roll out the puff pastry on a floured surface. Spread the mushroom mixture over the beef and wrap it tightly in the pastry.
6. Brush the pastry with beaten egg and bake for 25-30 minutes, or until the pastry is golden brown.
7. Let it rest before slicing and serving.

Fried Chicken with Gravy

Ingredients:

For the Chicken:

- 4 chicken thighs or breasts, skin-on
- 1 cup buttermilk
- 1 cup all-purpose flour
- 1 teaspoon paprika
- 1 teaspoon garlic powder
- 1/2 teaspoon onion powder
- Salt and pepper to taste
- Vegetable oil for frying

For the Gravy:

- 2 tablespoons butter
- 2 tablespoons all-purpose flour
- 2 cups chicken broth
- Salt and pepper to taste

Instructions:

1. In a bowl, soak the chicken in buttermilk for at least 30 minutes.
2. In a separate bowl, combine the flour, paprika, garlic powder, onion powder, salt, and pepper.
3. Heat vegetable oil in a deep skillet over medium-high heat.
4. Dredge each chicken piece in the flour mixture, pressing to coat evenly.
5. Fry the chicken for 6-8 minutes per side, until golden and crispy, and the internal temperature reaches 165°F (74°C).
6. Remove the chicken and drain on paper towels.
7. For the gravy, melt butter in a saucepan over medium heat. Stir in the flour and cook for 1-2 minutes.
8. Gradually whisk in the chicken broth and cook until thickened, about 3-5 minutes.
9. Season the gravy with salt and pepper and serve over the fried chicken.

Chicken Parmesan

Ingredients:

- 4 boneless, skinless chicken breasts
- 1 cup breadcrumbs
- 1/2 cup grated Parmesan cheese
- 1 teaspoon dried oregano
- 1 teaspoon garlic powder
- 1 egg, beaten
- 1 cup marinara sauce
- 1 1/2 cups shredded mozzarella cheese
- Olive oil for frying
- Fresh basil for garnish (optional)

Instructions:

1. Preheat the oven to 375°F (190°C).
2. Mix the breadcrumbs, Parmesan cheese, oregano, and garlic powder in a shallow dish.
3. Dip each chicken breast in the beaten egg, then coat with the breadcrumb mixture.
4. Heat olive oil in a large skillet over medium heat. Fry the chicken for 3-4 minutes per side, until golden brown.
5. Place the fried chicken on a baking sheet. Top each breast with marinara sauce and mozzarella cheese.
6. Bake in the oven for 20 minutes, or until the chicken is cooked through and the cheese is melted.
7. Garnish with fresh basil and serve.

Eggplant Parmesan

Ingredients:

- 2 medium eggplants, sliced into 1/2-inch thick rounds
- 1 cup breadcrumbs
- 1/2 cup grated Parmesan cheese
- 1 teaspoon dried oregano
- 1 teaspoon garlic powder
- 2 eggs, beaten
- 2 cups marinara sauce
- 1 1/2 cups shredded mozzarella cheese
- Olive oil for frying
- Fresh basil for garnish (optional)

Instructions:

1. Preheat the oven to 375°F (190°C).
2. Mix the breadcrumbs, Parmesan cheese, oregano, and garlic powder in a shallow dish.
3. Dip each eggplant slice in the beaten egg, then coat with the breadcrumb mixture.
4. Heat olive oil in a skillet over medium heat. Fry the eggplant slices for 2-3 minutes per side, until golden brown.
5. Place the fried eggplant slices in a baking dish. Top each slice with marinara sauce and mozzarella cheese.
6. Bake in the oven for 20 minutes, until the cheese is melted and bubbly.
7. Garnish with fresh basil and serve.

Beef and Bean Burritos

Ingredients:

- 1 pound ground beef
- 1 can (15 ounces) black beans, drained and rinsed
- 1 packet taco seasoning
- 1/2 cup salsa
- 6 flour tortillas
- 1 cup shredded cheddar cheese
- 1/2 cup sour cream
- 1/2 cup chopped lettuce
- 1/2 cup diced tomatoes

Instructions:

1. In a large skillet, cook the ground beef over medium heat until browned. Drain excess fat.
2. Stir in the taco seasoning and salsa. Simmer for 5 minutes.
3. In the center of each tortilla, spoon a portion of the beef mixture, then top with black beans, shredded cheese, sour cream, lettuce, and tomatoes.
4. Roll up the tortillas, folding in the sides as you go.
5. Serve warm.

Grilled Cheese and Tomato Soup

Ingredients:

For the Grilled Cheese:

- 8 slices of bread
- 4 tablespoons butter, softened
- 4 slices of cheddar cheese

For the Tomato Soup:

- 1 can (28 ounces) crushed tomatoes
- 1 cup chicken or vegetable broth
- 1/2 cup heavy cream
- 1 teaspoon sugar
- 1/2 teaspoon dried basil
- Salt and pepper to taste

Instructions:

1. For the soup, combine the crushed tomatoes, broth, heavy cream, sugar, basil, salt, and pepper in a pot. Simmer over low heat for 20 minutes.
2. For the grilled cheese, butter one side of each slice of bread.
3. Heat a skillet over medium heat. Place a slice of bread, butter-side down, in the skillet and add a slice of cheese.
4. Top with another slice of bread, butter-side up. Grill for 3-4 minutes on each side, until golden and the cheese is melted.
5. Serve the grilled cheese alongside the tomato soup.

Clam Chowder

Ingredients:

- 2 cans (6.5 ounces each) minced clams, drained and juice reserved
- 1 cup diced potatoes
- 1/2 cup diced celery
- 1/2 cup diced onion
- 1/4 cup butter
- 2 cups heavy cream
- 1 cup milk
- 1/4 cup flour
- Salt and pepper to taste

Instructions:

1. In a large pot, melt the butter over medium heat. Add the onion, celery, and potatoes. Cook for 5 minutes until softened.
2. Sprinkle the flour over the vegetables and stir to coat. Cook for 2 minutes.
3. Gradually add the clam juice, stirring to avoid lumps. Add the milk and heavy cream, and bring to a simmer.
4. Add the clams and cook for an additional 10-15 minutes, until the chowder thickens.
5. Season with salt and pepper and serve.

Pork Schnitzel with Cabbage

Ingredients:

- 4 pork cutlets
- 1 cup breadcrumbs
- 1/2 cup all-purpose flour
- 2 eggs, beaten
- 1/2 teaspoon salt
- 1/2 teaspoon pepper
- 2 tablespoons vegetable oil
- 2 cups shredded cabbage
- 1 tablespoon vinegar
- 1 tablespoon sugar

Instructions:

1. Season the pork cutlets with salt and pepper. Dredge them in flour, dip in beaten eggs, and coat with breadcrumbs.
2. Heat vegetable oil in a large skillet over medium-high heat. Fry the cutlets for 4-5 minutes per side until golden and crispy.
3. For the cabbage, combine shredded cabbage, vinegar, and sugar in a skillet. Cook over medium heat for 5-7 minutes until tender.
4. Serve the schnitzel with the sautéed cabbage.

Baked French Onion Soup

Ingredients:

- 4 large onions, thinly sliced
- 4 cups beef broth
- 1/4 cup butter
- 1 tablespoon flour
- 1/2 teaspoon thyme
- 1/2 teaspoon salt
- 1/4 teaspoon pepper
- 4 slices French bread
- 1 1/2 cups shredded Gruyère cheese

Instructions:

1. In a large pot, melt butter over medium heat. Add the onions and cook for 20 minutes, stirring occasionally, until caramelized.
2. Stir in the flour, thyme, salt, and pepper. Add the beef broth and simmer for 20 minutes.
3. Preheat the oven to 350°F (175°C). Place the French bread on a baking sheet and toast until golden.
4. Ladle the soup into oven-safe bowls, top with a slice of toasted bread, and sprinkle with Gruyère cheese.
5. Broil in the oven for 5 minutes, until the cheese is melted and bubbly.

Roasted Chicken with Root Vegetables

Ingredients:

- 1 whole chicken (about 4 pounds)
- 2 tablespoons olive oil
- 1 teaspoon garlic powder
- 1 teaspoon dried rosemary
- 1 teaspoon thyme
- 4 carrots, peeled and chopped
- 4 potatoes, peeled and chopped
- 2 onions, peeled and quartered

Instructions:

1. Preheat the oven to 400°F (200°C).
2. Rub the chicken with olive oil, garlic powder, rosemary, thyme, salt, and pepper.
3. Place the chicken on a roasting rack in a baking dish. Surround with the chopped vegetables.
4. Roast for 1.5 hours, or until the chicken reaches an internal temperature of 165°F (74°C).
5. Let the chicken rest before serving.

Sweet and Sour Meatballs

Ingredients:

- 1 pound ground beef
- 1/2 cup breadcrumbs
- 1 egg
- 1 teaspoon garlic powder
- 1/4 teaspoon salt
- 1/4 teaspoon pepper
- 1/2 cup ketchup
- 1/4 cup vinegar
- 1/4 cup brown sugar

Instructions:

1. Preheat the oven to 375°F (190°C). In a bowl, combine the ground beef, breadcrumbs, egg, garlic powder, salt, and pepper. Form into meatballs.
2. Place the meatballs on a baking sheet and bake for 20 minutes.
3. In a saucepan, combine the ketchup, vinegar, and brown sugar. Bring to a simmer and cook for 5 minutes.
4. Toss the meatballs in the sweet and sour sauce and serve.

Baked Mac and Cheese with Bacon

Ingredients:

- 8 ounces elbow macaroni
- 1 tablespoon butter
- 2 tablespoons all-purpose flour
- 2 cups milk
- 2 cups shredded sharp cheddar cheese
- 1 cup shredded mozzarella cheese
- 1/2 teaspoon mustard powder
- Salt and pepper to taste
- 1/2 cup breadcrumbs
- 6 slices bacon, cooked and crumbled
- 1 tablespoon butter (for topping)

Instructions:

1. Preheat the oven to 350°F (175°C).
2. Cook the elbow macaroni according to the package instructions, drain, and set aside.
3. In a saucepan, melt butter over medium heat. Stir in the flour and cook for 2 minutes to create a roux.
4. Gradually whisk in the milk, and cook until the sauce thickens (about 5 minutes).
5. Remove the saucepan from heat, then stir in the cheddar cheese, mozzarella cheese, mustard powder, salt, and pepper until smooth.
6. Combine the cooked macaroni, cheese sauce, and crumbled bacon in a large baking dish.
7. Sprinkle breadcrumbs on top, and dot with butter.
8. Bake for 25 minutes until golden and bubbly. Serve warm.

Cozy Risotto with Mushrooms

Ingredients:

- 1 cup Arborio rice
- 2 tablespoons butter
- 1 small onion, finely chopped
- 2 cups sliced mushrooms (cremini or white)
- 1/2 cup white wine
- 4 cups chicken or vegetable broth (kept warm)
- 1/2 cup grated Parmesan cheese
- Salt and pepper to taste
- Fresh parsley for garnish

Instructions:

1. In a large skillet, melt the butter over medium heat. Add the onion and cook until softened, about 3 minutes.
2. Add the mushrooms and cook for an additional 5 minutes until they release their moisture and become tender.
3. Stir in the Arborio rice and cook for 1-2 minutes, allowing the rice to lightly toast.
4. Pour in the white wine and cook until mostly absorbed by the rice.
5. Gradually add the warm broth, one ladle at a time, stirring frequently and allowing the liquid to be absorbed before adding more.
6. Continue until the rice is creamy and tender, about 18-20 minutes.
7. Stir in the Parmesan cheese, and season with salt and pepper.
8. Garnish with fresh parsley and serve warm.

Braised Lamb Shanks

Ingredients:

- 4 lamb shanks
- 2 tablespoons olive oil
- 1 onion, chopped
- 2 carrots, chopped
- 3 garlic cloves, minced
- 1 cup red wine
- 2 cups beef broth
- 2 teaspoons fresh rosemary, chopped
- 1 teaspoon thyme
- Salt and pepper to taste

Instructions:

1. Preheat the oven to 325°F (165°C).
2. In a large Dutch oven, heat olive oil over medium-high heat. Brown the lamb shanks on all sides, about 8-10 minutes. Remove and set aside.
3. In the same pot, sauté the onion, carrots, and garlic until softened, about 5 minutes.
4. Add the red wine, scraping up any brown bits from the bottom of the pot. Let the wine reduce for 3 minutes.
5. Return the lamb shanks to the pot, add the beef broth, rosemary, thyme, salt, and pepper.
6. Cover the pot and place it in the oven. Braise the lamb for 2 to 2 1/2 hours, until tender.
7. Serve the lamb shanks with the braised vegetables and sauce from the pot.

Sloppy Joes

Ingredients:

- 1 pound ground beef
- 1 small onion, chopped
- 1 green bell pepper, chopped
- 1 cup ketchup
- 1 tablespoon Worcestershire sauce
- 1 tablespoon mustard
- 2 tablespoons brown sugar
- Salt and pepper to taste
- 4 hamburger buns

Instructions:

1. In a large skillet, cook the ground beef over medium heat until browned, about 5-7 minutes. Drain excess fat.
2. Add the chopped onion and bell pepper to the skillet and cook for 3-4 minutes until softened.
3. Stir in the ketchup, Worcestershire sauce, mustard, brown sugar, salt, and pepper. Simmer for 10-15 minutes until the sauce thickens.
4. Spoon the mixture onto the hamburger buns and serve hot.

Cornbread with Chili

Ingredients:

For the Cornbread:

- 1 cup cornmeal
- 1 cup all-purpose flour
- 1/4 cup sugar
- 1 tablespoon baking powder
- 1/2 teaspoon salt
- 1 cup milk
- 2 eggs
- 1/4 cup butter, melted

For the Chili:

- 1 pound ground beef
- 1 onion, chopped
- 1 can (15 ounces) kidney beans, drained and rinsed
- 1 can (15 ounces) diced tomatoes
- 2 tablespoons chili powder
- 1 teaspoon cumin
- Salt and pepper to taste

Instructions:

1. Preheat the oven to 425°F (220°C).
2. In a large bowl, mix together cornmeal, flour, sugar, baking powder, and salt. In another bowl, whisk together milk, eggs, and melted butter.
3. Combine both mixtures and stir until smooth.
4. Pour the batter into a greased 9x9-inch baking dish. Bake for 20-25 minutes, until golden and a toothpick comes out clean.
5. For the chili, cook the ground beef in a large pot over medium heat until browned. Drain excess fat.
6. Add the chopped onion and cook for 3-4 minutes until softened.
7. Stir in the beans, tomatoes, chili powder, cumin, salt, and pepper. Simmer for 20 minutes.
8. Serve the chili with a side of freshly baked cornbread.

Baked Chicken Thighs with Garlic Butter

Ingredients:

- 4 bone-in, skin-on chicken thighs
- 4 tablespoons butter, melted
- 4 garlic cloves, minced
- 1 teaspoon dried thyme
- 1 teaspoon dried rosemary
- Salt and pepper to taste

Instructions:

1. Preheat the oven to 400°F (200°C).
2. In a small bowl, mix the melted butter with minced garlic, thyme, rosemary, salt, and pepper.
3. Place the chicken thighs on a baking sheet and brush with the garlic butter mixture.
4. Bake for 35-40 minutes, or until the internal temperature reaches 165°F (74°C) and the skin is crispy.
5. Serve warm.

Stuffed Mushrooms with Cream Cheese

Ingredients:

- 12 large mushrooms, stems removed
- 8 ounces cream cheese, softened
- 1/4 cup grated Parmesan cheese
- 2 tablespoons breadcrumbs
- 2 tablespoons fresh parsley, chopped
- 1/2 teaspoon garlic powder
- Salt and pepper to taste
- Olive oil for greasing

Instructions:

1. Preheat the oven to 350°F (175°C).
2. Grease a baking sheet with olive oil. Place the mushroom caps on the sheet, hollow-side up.
3. In a bowl, combine the cream cheese, Parmesan cheese, breadcrumbs, parsley, garlic powder, salt, and pepper.
4. Stuff each mushroom cap with the cream cheese mixture.
5. Bake for 20-25 minutes, until the mushrooms are tender and the filling is golden.
6. Serve warm.

Cabbage Rolls

Ingredients:

- 1 large head of cabbage
- 1 lb ground beef or pork
- 1 cup cooked rice
- 1 onion, chopped
- 2 cloves garlic, minced
- 1 can (15 oz) tomato sauce
- 1 can (14 oz) crushed tomatoes
- 2 tablespoons brown sugar
- 1 tablespoon Worcestershire sauce
- 1 teaspoon paprika
- Salt and pepper to taste

Instructions:

1. Preheat the oven to 350°F (175°C).
2. Bring a large pot of water to a boil. Carefully remove the cabbage leaves one by one, blanching them for about 2 minutes until softened. Drain and set aside.
3. In a large skillet, cook the ground beef (or pork) with the chopped onion and garlic until browned. Drain any excess fat.
4. Stir in the cooked rice, tomato sauce, crushed tomatoes, brown sugar, Worcestershire sauce, paprika, salt, and pepper.
5. Place a generous spoonful of the mixture onto each cabbage leaf, then roll up tightly, folding in the sides as you go.
6. Place the cabbage rolls in a baking dish. Pour any remaining tomato sauce over the top and cover with foil.
7. Bake for 1 hour, removing the foil for the last 10 minutes to brown the top.

Baked Salmon with Lemon Dill Sauce

Ingredients:

- 4 salmon fillets
- 2 tablespoons olive oil
- Salt and pepper to taste
- 1 lemon, sliced
- 1/2 cup sour cream
- 2 tablespoons fresh dill, chopped
- 1 tablespoon Dijon mustard
- 1 tablespoon lemon juice

Instructions:

1. Preheat the oven to 375°F (190°C).
2. Place the salmon fillets on a baking sheet lined with parchment paper. Drizzle with olive oil and season with salt and pepper. Place lemon slices on top of the salmon.
3. Bake for 15-20 minutes, or until the salmon is cooked through and flakes easily with a fork.
4. In a small bowl, mix together sour cream, fresh dill, Dijon mustard, and lemon juice to make the sauce.
5. Serve the baked salmon with the lemon dill sauce on top or on the side.

Chicken Enchiladas with Sour Cream

Ingredients:

- 3 cups cooked, shredded chicken
- 10 flour tortillas
- 1 can (10 oz) enchilada sauce
- 1 cup shredded cheddar cheese
- 1 cup shredded Monterey Jack cheese
- 1/2 cup sour cream
- 1 small onion, chopped
- 1 tablespoon olive oil
- Salt and pepper to taste

Instructions:

1. Preheat the oven to 350°F (175°C).
2. In a skillet, heat olive oil over medium heat. Add chopped onions and cook until soft, about 3-4 minutes.
3. Add the shredded chicken, half of the enchilada sauce, and salt and pepper. Stir to combine and heat through.
4. In a baking dish, spread a thin layer of enchilada sauce on the bottom.
5. Place a spoonful of the chicken mixture into each tortilla, roll it up, and place seam-side down in the baking dish.
6. Pour the remaining enchilada sauce over the top of the rolls, then sprinkle with both cheeses.
7. Bake for 20-25 minutes, until the cheese is melted and bubbly.
8. Serve with a dollop of sour cream.

Creamed Spinach

Ingredients:

- 1 lb fresh spinach, washed and chopped
- 2 tablespoons butter
- 1 small onion, chopped
- 2 cloves garlic, minced
- 1 cup heavy cream
- 1/2 teaspoon nutmeg
- Salt and pepper to taste
- 1/2 cup grated Parmesan cheese

Instructions:

1. In a large skillet, melt the butter over medium heat. Add the chopped onion and garlic and cook until softened, about 3-4 minutes.
2. Add the spinach to the skillet and cook until wilted, about 5-7 minutes.
3. Stir in the heavy cream, nutmeg, salt, and pepper. Let the mixture simmer for 5-10 minutes until it thickens.
4. Stir in the grated Parmesan cheese and adjust seasoning as needed.
5. Serve the creamed spinach warm.

Poutine

Ingredients:

- 4 cups frozen French fries (or homemade)
- 2 cups cheese curds
- 1 1/2 cups brown gravy (store-bought or homemade)

Instructions:

1. Cook the French fries according to the package instructions, or prepare homemade fries and bake or fry them.
2. While the fries are cooking, heat the brown gravy in a saucepan over medium heat.
3. Once the fries are ready, place them on a serving platter. Sprinkle with cheese curds, ensuring they are spread evenly.
4. Pour the hot brown gravy over the fries and cheese curds.
5. Serve immediately while hot and enjoy this classic Canadian dish.

Slow-Cooked Pork Carnitas

Ingredients:

- 3-4 lbs pork shoulder
- 1 onion, quartered
- 4 cloves garlic, smashed
- 1 orange, halved
- 1 teaspoon ground cumin
- 1 teaspoon chili powder
- 1 teaspoon oregano
- 1 bay leaf
- Salt and pepper to taste
- Tortillas and toppings (such as cilantro, lime, salsa, etc.)

Instructions:

1. In a slow cooker, place the pork shoulder, onion, garlic, orange, cumin, chili powder, oregano, bay leaf, salt, and pepper.
2. Squeeze the juice from the orange halves over the pork and add the halves into the slow cooker.

3. Cover and cook on low for 6-8 hours, or until the pork is fork-tender and shreds easily.
4. Remove the pork from the slow cooker and shred with two forks.
5. Serve the carnitas in tortillas with your favorite toppings.

Homemade Biscuits with Gravy

Ingredients:

For the Biscuits:

- 2 cups all-purpose flour
- 2 1/2 teaspoons baking powder
- 1/2 teaspoon salt
- 1/4 cup butter, cold and cubed
- 3/4 cup milk

For the Gravy:

- 1 lb breakfast sausage, crumbled
- 2 tablespoons flour
- 2 cups milk
- Salt and pepper to taste

Instructions:

1. Preheat the oven to 450°F (230°C).
2. In a bowl, combine the flour, baking powder, and salt. Cut in the cold butter until the mixture resembles coarse crumbs.
3. Gradually stir in the milk to form a dough. Do not overmix.
4. Turn the dough onto a lightly floured surface and roll it out to about 1-inch thickness. Cut out biscuits using a round cutter.
5. Place the biscuits on a baking sheet and bake for 10-12 minutes, until golden brown.
6. For the gravy, cook the sausage in a skillet over medium heat until browned. Remove and set aside.
7. In the same skillet, whisk in flour and cook for 1 minute. Gradually add the milk, stirring constantly until the gravy thickens.

8. Return the sausage to the skillet and stir to combine. Season with salt and pepper.
9. Serve the biscuits with the sausage gravy poured over the top.

www.ingramcontent.com/pod-product-compliance
Lightning Source LLC
LaVergne TN
LVHW081325060526
838201LV00055B/2457